CATO

A Tragedy

JOSEPH ADDISON

CONTENTS

DRAMATIS PERSONÆ

Cato, Marcus Portius Cato Uticensis, or Cato the Younger. Roman senator, governor of Utica, and champion of Roman Republicanism in opposition to Julius Caesar.

Portius, Son of Cato, twin of Marcus.

Marcus, Son of Cato, twin of Portius.

Sempronius, Senior Roman Senator.

Juba, Exiled prince of Numidia (a province in North Africa recently conquered by Rome). Friend and ally of Cato.

Syphax, Juba's servant.

Lucius, Senior Roman Senator.

Decius, Senior Roman statesman, ally of Caesar.

Lucia, Daughter of Lucius. Friend of Marcia and Portius.

Marcia, Daughter of Cato.

Mutineers, Guards, etc.

SCENE—*The Governor's Palace in Utica.*

ACT THE FIRST

Scene I.
A Hall.
Enter Portius *and* Marcus.

Portius. The dawn is overcast, the morning
    low'rs,
And heavily in clouds brings on the day,
The great, the important day, big with
    the fate
Of Cato and of Rome——Our father's death
Would fill up all the guilt of civil war,
And close the scene of blood. Already Cæsar
Has ravaged more than half the globe,
    and sees
Mankind grown thin by his destructive
    sword:
Should he go farther, numbers would be
    wanting
To form new battles, and support his crimes.
Ye gods, what havoc does ambition make
Among your works!

Marcus. Thy steady temper, Portius,
Can look on guilt, rebellion, fraud, and
          Cæsar,
In the calm lights of mild philosophy;
I'm tortured e'en to madness, when I think
On the proud victor—ev'ry time he's named,
Pharsalia rises to my view!—I see
Th' insulting tyrant, prancing o'er the field,
Strew'd with Rome's citizens, and drench'd
          in slaughter;
His horse's hoofs wet with patrician blood!
Oh, Portius! is there not some chosen curse,
Some hidden thunder in the stores of
          Heav'n,
Red with uncommon wrath, to blast the man
Who owes his greatness to his country's
          ruin?

Portius. Believe me, Marcus, 'tis an impious
          greatness,
And mix'd with too much horror to be
          envied:
How does the lustre of our father's actions,
Through the dark cloud of ills that
          cover him,
Break out, and burn with more triumphant
          brightness!
His sufferings shine, and spread a glory
          round him;
Greatly unfortunate, he fights the cause
Of honour, virtue, liberty, and Rome.
His sword ne'er fell, but on the guilty head;
Oppression, tyranny, and pow'r usurp'd,

Draw all the vengeance of his arm upon
them.

Marcus. Who knows not this? but what can
Cato do
Against a world, a base, degenerate world,
That courts the yoke, and bows the neck to
Cæsar?
Pent up in Utica, he vainly forms
A poor epitome of Roman greatness,
And, cover'd with Numidian guards, directs
A feeble army, and an empty senate,
Remnants of mighty battles fought in vain.
By Heav'n, such virtue, join'd with such
success,
Distracts my very soul! Our father's fortune
Would almost tempt us to renounce his
precepts.

Portius. Remember what our father oft has
told us:
The ways of Heav'n are dark and intricate,
Puzzled in mazes, and perplex'd with errors;
Our understanding traces them in vain,
Lost and bewilder'd in the fruitless search;
Nor sees with how much art the windings
run,
Nor where the regular confusion ends.

Marcus. These are suggestions of a mind at
ease:—
Oh, Portius! didst thou taste but half the
griefs

That wring my soul, thou couldst not talk
    thus coldly.
Passion unpitied, and successless love,
Plant daggers in my heart, and aggravate
My other griefs.—Were but my Lucia
    kind——

Portius. Thou see'st not that thy brother is
    thy rival;
But I must hide it, for I know thy temper.
    [*Aside.*
Behold young Juba, the Numidian prince,
With how much care he forms himself to
    glory,
And breaks the fierceness of his native
    temper,
To copy out our father's bright example.
He loves our sister Marcia, greatly loves her;
His eyes, his looks, his actions, all betray it;
But still the smother'd fondness burns
    within him;
When most it swells, and labours for a vent,
The sense of honour, and desire of fame,
Drive the big passion back into his heart.
What! shall an African, shall Juba's heir,
Reproach great Cato's son, and show the
    world
A virtue wanting in a Roman soul?

Marcus. Portius, no more! your words leave
    stings behind them.
Whene'er did Juba, or did Portius, show
A virtue that has cast me at a distance,

And thrown me out in the pursuits of
    honour?

Portius. Marcus, I know thy gen'rous temper
    well;
Fling but the appearance of dishonour on it,
It straight takes fire, and mounts into a blaze.

Marcus. A brother's suff'rings claim a
    brother's pity.

Portius. Heav'n knows, I pity thee——Behold
    my eyes,
Ev'n whilst I speak—Do they not swim in
    tears?
Were but my heart as naked to thy view,
Marcus would see it bleed in his behalf.

Marcus. Why then dost treat me with
    rebukes, instead
Of kind condoling cares, and friendly
    sorrow?

Portius. Oh, Marcus! did I know the way
    to ease
Thy troubled heart, and mitigate thy pains,
Marcus, believe me, I could die to do it.

Marcus. Thou best of brothers, and thou best
    of friends!
Pardon a weak distemper'd soul, that swells
With sudden gusts, and sinks as soon in
    calms,

The sport of passions. But Sempronius
    comes:
He must not find this softness hanging
    on me.

                            [*Exit* Marcus.

          Enter Sempronius.

Sempronius. Conspiracies no sooner should
    be form'd
Than executed. What means Portius here?
I like not that cold youth. I must dissemble,
And speak a language foreign to my heart.
    [*Aside.*
Good-morrow, Portius; let us once embrace,
Once more embrace, while yet we both are
    free.
To-morrow, should we thus express our
    friendship,
Each might receive a slave into his arms;
This sun, perhaps, this morning sun's the last
That e'er shall rise on Roman liberty.

Portius. My father has this morning call'd
    together
To this poor hall, his little Roman senate,
(The leavings of Pharsalia) to consult
If he can yet oppose the mighty torrent
That bears down Rome and all her gods
    before it,
Or must at length give up the world to
    Cæsar.

Sempronius. Not all the pomp and majesty
    of Rome
Can raise her senate more than Cato's
    presence.
His virtues render our assembly awful,
They strike with something like religious
    fear,
And make even Cæsar tremble at the head
Of armies flush'd with conquest. Oh, my
    Portius!
Could I but call that wond'rous man my
    father,
Would but thy sister Marcia be propitious
To thy friend's vows, I might be blest indeed!

Portius. Alas, Sempronius! wouldst thou talk
    of love
To Marcia, whilst her father's life's in danger?
Thou might'st as well court the pale,
    trembling vestal,
When she beholds the holy flame expiring.

Sempronius. The more I see the wonders of
    thy race,
The more I'm charm'd. Thou must take
    heed, my Portius;
The world has all its eyes on Cato's son;
Thy father's merit sets thee up to view,
And shows thee in the fairest point of light,
To make thy virtues or thy faults
    conspicuous.

Portius. Well dost thou seem to check my
    ling'ring here

In this important hour—I'll straight away,
And while the fathers of the senate meet
In close debate, to weigh th' events of war,
I'll animate the soldiers' drooping courage
With love of freedom and contempt of life;
I'll thunder in their ears their country's
    cause,
And try to rouse up all that's Roman in them.
'Tis not in mortals to command success,
But we'll do more, Sempronius—we'll
    deserve it.[*Exit.*

Sempronius. Curse on the stripling! how he
    apes his sire!
Ambitiously sententious—But I wonder
Old Syphax comes not; his Numidian genius
Is well disposed to mischief, were he prompt
And eager on it; but he must be spurr'd,
And every moment quicken'd to the course.
Cato has used me ill; he has refused
His daughter Marcia to my ardent vows.
Besides, his baffled arms, and ruin'd cause,
Are bars to my ambition. Cæsar's favour,
That show'rs down greatness on his friends,
    will raise me
To Rome's first honours. If I give up Cato,
I claim, in my reward, his captive daughter.
But Syphax comes——

Enter Syphax.

Syphax. Sempronius, all is ready;
I've sounded my Numidians, man by man,
And find them ripe for a revolt: they all

Complain aloud of Cato's discipline,
And wait but the command to change their
    master.

Sempronius. Believe me, Syphax, there's no
    time to waste;
Ev'n while we speak, our conqueror
    comes on,
And gathers ground upon us every moment.
Alas! thou know'st not Cæsar's active soul,
With what a dreadful course he rushes on
From war to war. In vain has nature form'd
Mountains and oceans t'oppose his passage;
He bounds o'er all.
One day more
Will set the victor thund'ring at our gates.
But, tell me, hast thou yet drawn o'er young
    Juba?
That still would recommend thee more to
    Cæsar,
And challenge better terms.

Syphax. Alas! he's lost!
He's lost, Sempronius; all his thoughts
    are full
Of Cato's virtues—But I'll try once more
(For every instant I expect him here)
If yet I can subdue those stubborn principles
Of faith and honour, and I know not what,
That have corrupted his Numidian temper,
And struck th' infection into all his soul.

Sempronius. Be sure to press upon him every
    motive.

Juba's surrender, since his father's death,
Would give up Afric into Cæsar's hands,
And make him lord of half the burning zone.

Syphax. But is it true, Sempronius, that your
    senate
Is call'd together? Gods! thou must be
    cautious;
Cato has piercing eyes, and will discern
Our frauds, unless they're cover'd thick
    with art.

Sempronius. Let me alone, good Syphax, I'll
    conceal
My thoughts in passion ('tis the surest way);
I'll bellow out for Rome, and for my country,
And mouth at Cæsar, till I shake the senate.
Your cold hypocrisy's a stale device,
A worn-out trick: wouldst thou be thought in
    earnest,
Clothe thy feign'd zeal in rage, in fire, in fury!

Syphax. In troth, thou'rt able to instruct grey
    hairs,
And teach the wily African deceit.

Sempronius. Once more be sure to try thy
    skill on Juba.
Remember, Syphax, we must work in haste;
Oh, think what anxious moments pass
    between
The birth of plots, and their last fatal
    periods!
Oh, 'tis a dreadful interval of time,

Fill'd up with horror all, and big with death!
Destruction hangs on every word we speak,
On every thought, till the concluding stroke
Determines all, and closes our design. [*Exit.*

Syphax. I'll try if yet I can reduce to reason
This headstrong youth, and make him spurn
        at Cato.
The time is short; Cæsar comes rushing
        on us—
But hold! young Juba sees me, and
        approaches!

Enter Juba.

Juba. Syphax, I joy to meet thee thus alone.
I have observed of late thy looks are fall'n,
O'ercast with gloomy cares and discontent;
Then tell me, Syphax, I conjure thee, tell me,
What are the thoughts that knit thy brow in
        frowns,
And turn thine eye thus coldly on thy
        prince?

Syphax. 'Tis not my talent to conceal my
        thoughts,
Or carry smiles and sunshine in my face,
When discontent sits heavy at my heart;
I have not yet so much the Roman in me.

Juba. Why dost thou cast out such
        ungenerous terms
Against the lords and sov'reigns of the
        world?

Dost thou not see mankind fall down before
    them,
And own the force of their superior virtue?
Is there a nation in the wilds of Afric,
Amidst our barren rocks and burning sands,
That does not tremble at the Roman name?

Syphax. Gods! where's the worth that sets
    these people up
Above your own Numidia's tawny sons?
Do they with tougher sinews bend the bow?
Or flies the javelin swifter to its mark,
Launch'd from the vigour of a Roman arm?
Who like our active African instructs
The fiery steed, and trains him to his hand?
Or guides in troops th' embattled elephant
Laden with war? These, these are arts, my
    prince,
In which your Zama does not stoop to Rome.

Juba. These all are virtues of a meaner rank:
Perfections that are placed in bones and
    nerves.
A Roman soul is bent on higher views;
Turn up thy eyes to Cato;
There may'st thou see to what a godlike
    height
The Roman virtues lift up mortal man.
While good, and just, and anxious for his
    friends,
He's still severely bent against himself;
And when his fortune sets before him all
The pomps and pleasures that his soul can
    wish,

His rigid virtue will accept of none.

Syphax. Believe me, prince, there's not an African
That traverses our vast Numidian deserts
In quest of prey, and lives upon his bow,
But better practises those boasted virtues.
Coarse are his meals, the fortune of the chase;
Amidst the running stream he slakes his thirst;
Toils all the day, and, at the approach of night,
On the first friendly bank he throws him down,
Or rests his head upon a rock till morn;
Then rises fresh, pursues his wonted game,
And if the following day he chance to find
A new repast, or an untasted spring,
Blesses his stars, and thinks it luxury.

Juba. Thy prejudices, Syphax, won't discern
What virtues grow from ignorance and choice,
Nor how the hero differs from the brute.
Where shall we find the man that bears affliction,
Great and majestic in his griefs, like Cato?
How does he rise against a load of woes,
And thank the gods that threw the weight upon him!

Syphax. 'Tis pride, rank pride, and haughtiness of soul;

I think the Romans call it stoicism.
Had not your royal father thought so highly
Of Roman virtue, and of Cato's cause,
He had not fall'n by a slave's hand
    inglorious.

Juba. Why dost thou call my sorrows up
    afresh?
My father's name brings tears into my eyes.

Syphax. Oh, that you'd profit by your father's
    ills!

Juba. What wouldst thou have me do?

Syphax. Abandon Cato.

Juba. Syphax, I should be more than twice an
    orphan
By such a loss.

Syphax. Ay, there's the tie that binds you!
You long to call him father. Marcia's charms
Work in your heart unseen, and plead for
    Cato.
No wonder you are deaf to all I say.

Juba. Syphax, your zeal becomes
    importunate;
I've hitherto permitted it to rave,
And talk at large; but learn to keep it in,
Lest it should take more freedom than I'll
    give it.

Syphax. Sir, your great father never used me
  thus.
Alas, he's dead! but can you e'er forget
The tender sorrows,
And repeated blessings,
Which you drew from him in your last
  farewell?
The good old king, at parting, wrung my
  hand,
(His eyes brimful of tears) then sighing cried,
Pr'ythee be careful of my son!——His grief
Swell'd up so high, he could not utter more.

Juba. Alas! thy story melts away my soul!
That best of fathers! how shall I discharge
The gratitude and duty that I owe him?

Syphax. By laying up his counsels in your
  heart.

Juba. His counsels bade me yield to thy
  direction:
Then, Syphax, chide me in severest terms,
Vent all thy passion, and I'll stand its shock,
Calm and unruffled as a summer sea,
When not a breath of wind flies o'er its
  surface.

Syphax. Alas! my prince, I'd guide you to
  your safety.

Juba. I do believe thou wouldst; but tell
  me how?

Syphax. Fly from the fate that follows
    Cæsar's foes.

Juba. My father scorn'd to do it.

Syphax. And therefore died.

Juba. Better to die ten thousand thousand
    deaths,
Than wound my honour.

Syphax. Rather say, your love.

Juba. Syphax, I've promised to preserve my
    temper;
Why wilt thou urge me to confess a flame
I long have stifled, and would fain conceal?

Syphax. Believe me, prince, though hard to
    conquer love,
'Tis easy to divert and break its force.
Absence might cure it, or a second mistress
Light up another flame, and put out this.
The glowing dames of Zama's royal court
Have faces flush'd with more exalted charms;
Were you with these, my prince, you'd soon
    forget
The pale, unripen'd beauties of the north.

Juba. 'Tis not a set of features, or
    complexion,
The tincture of a skin, that I admire:
Beauty soon grows familiar to the lover,
Fades in his eye, and palls upon the sense.

The virtuous Marcia tow'rs above her sex:
True, she is fair (Oh, how divinely fair!),
But still the lovely maid improves her
    charms,
With inward greatness, unaffected wisdom,
And sanctity of manners; Cato's soul
Shines out in every thing she acts or speaks,
While winning mildness and attractive
    smiles
Dwell in her looks, and, with becoming
    grace,
Soften the rigour of her father's virtue.

Syphax. How does your tongue grow wanton
    in her praise!
But on my knees, I beg you would
    consider—

Juba. Ha! Syphax, is't not she?—She moves
    this way;
And with her Lucia, Lucius's fair daughter.
My heart beats thick—I pr'ythee, Syphax,
    leave me.

Syphax. Ten thousand curses fasten on them
    both!
Now will the woman, with a single glance,
Undo what I've been lab'ring all this while.
    [*Exit* Syphax.

        Enter Marcia *and* Lucia.

Juba. Hail, charming maid! How does thy
    beauty smooth

The face of war, and make even horror smile!
At sight of thee my heart shakes off its
    sorrows;
I feel a dawn of joy break in upon me,
And for a while forget th' approach of Cæsar.

Marcia. I should be grieved, young prince, to
    think my presence
Unbent your thoughts, and slacken'd them
    to arms,
While, warm with slaughter, our victorious
    foe
Threatens aloud, and calls you to the field.

Juba. Oh, Marcia, let me hope thy kind
    concerns
And gentle wishes follow me to battle!
The thought will give new vigour to my arm,
And strength and weight to my descending
    sword,
And drive it in a tempest on the foe.

Marcia. My pray'rs and wishes always shall
    attend
The friends of Rome, the glorious cause of
    virtue,
And men approved of by the gods and Cato.

Juba. That Juba may deserve thy pious cares,
I'll gaze for ever on thy godlike father,
Transplanting one by one, into my life,
His bright perfections, till I shine like him.

Marcia. My father never, at a time like this,

Would lay out his great soul in words, and
    waste
Such precious moments.

Juba. Thy reproofs are just,
Thou virtuous maid; I'll hasten to my troops,
And fire their languid souls with Cato's
    virtue.
If e'er I lead them to the field, when all
The war shall stand ranged in its just array,
And dreadful pomp, then will I think on
    thee;
Oh, lovely maid! then will I think on thee;
And, in the shock of charging hosts,
    remember
What glorious deeds should grace the man
    who hopes
For Marcia's love.[*Exit* Juba.

Lucius. Marcia, you're too severe;
How could you chide the young good-
    natured prince,
And drive him from you with so stern an air,
A prince that loves, and dotes on you to
    death?

Marcia. 'Tis therefore, Lucia, that I chide him
    from me;
His air, his voice, his looks, and honest soul,
Speak all so movingly in his behalf,
I dare not trust myself to hear him talk.

Lucius. Why will you fight against so sweet a
    passion,

And steel your heart to such a world of
    charms?

Marcia. How, Lucia! wouldst thou have me
    sink away
In pleasing dreams, and lose myself in love,
When ev'ry moment Cato's life's at stake?
Cæsar comes arm'd with terror and revenge,
And aims his thunder at my father's head.
Should not the sad occasion swallow up
My other cares?

Lucius. Why have I not this constancy of
    mind,
Who have so many griefs to try its force?
Sure, Nature form'd me of her softest mould,
Enfeebled all my soul with tender passions,
And sunk me ev'n below my own weak sex:
Pity and love, by turns, oppress my heart.

Marcia. Lucia, disburden all thy cares on me,
And let me share thy most retired distress.
Tell me, who raises up this conflict in thee?

Lucius. I need not blush to name them, when
    I tell thee
They're Marcia's brothers, and the sons of
    Cato.

Marcia. They both behold thee with their
    sister's eyes,
And often have reveal'd their passion to me.
But tell me, which of them is Lucia's choice?

Lucius. Suppose 'twere Portius, could you
    blame my choice?—
Oh, Portius, thou hast stolen away my soul!
Marcus is over warm, his fond complaints
Have so much earnestness and passion in
    them,
I hear him with a secret kind of horror,
And tremble at his vehemence of temper.

Marcia. Alas, poor youth!
How will thy coldness raise
Tempests and storms in his afflicted bosom!
I dread the consequence.

Lucius. You seem to plead
Against your brother Portius.

Marcia. Heav'n forbid.
Had Portius been the unsuccessful lover,
The same compassion would have fall'n
    on him.

Lucius. Was ever virgin love distress'd like
    mine!
Portius himself oft falls in tears before me
As if he mourn'd his rival's ill success;
Then bids me hide the motions of my heart,
Nor show which way it turns—so much he
    fears
The sad effect that it will have on Marcus.

Marcia. Let us not, Lucia, aggravate our
    sorrows,
But to the gods submit the event of things.

Our lives, discolour'd with our present woes,
May still grow bright, and smile with happier
    hours.
So the pure limpid stream, when foul with
    stains
Of rushing torrents and descending rains,
Works itself clear, and, as it runs, refines,
Till, by degrees, the floating mirror shines;
Reflects each flower that on the border
    grows,
And a new heav'n in its fair bosom shows.
    [*Exeunt.*

ACT THE SECOND

SCENE I.
The Senate sitting.
Flourish.
Enter Cato.

Cato. Fathers, we once again are met in
　　council;
Cæsar's approach has summon'd us together,
And Rome attends her fate from our
　　resolves.
How shall we treat this bold aspiring man?
Success still follows him, and backs his
　　crimes;
Pharsalia gave him Rome, Egypt has since
Received his yoke, and the whole Nile is
　　Cæsar's.
Why should I mention Juba's overthrow,
And Scipio's death? Numidia's burning sands
Still smoke with blood. 'Tis time we should
　　decree
What course to take. Our foe advances on us,
And envies us even Lybia's sultry deserts.

Fathers, pronounce your thoughts: are they
    still fix'd
To hold it out, and fight it to the last?
Or are your hearts subdued at length, and
    wrought,
By time and ill success, to a submission?
Sempronius, speak.

Sempronius. Gods! can a Roman senate long
    debate
Which of the two to chuse, slav'ry or death!
No; let us rise at once, gird on our swords,
And, at the head of our remaining troops,
Attack the foe, break through the thick array
Of his throng'd legions, and charge home
    upon him.
Perhaps some arm, more lucky than the
    rest,
May reach his heart, and free the world from
    bondage.
Rise, fathers, rise! 'tis Rome demands your
    help;
Rise, and revenge her slaughter'd citizens,
Or share their fate!—
To battle!
Great Pompey's shade complains that we are
    slow;
And Scipio's ghost walks unrevenged
    amongst us.

Cato. Let not a torrent of impetuous zeal
Transport thee thus beyond the bounds of
    reason;
True fortitude is seen in great exploits,

That justice warrants, and that wisdom
    guides;
All else is tow'ring phrensy and distraction.
Lucius, we next would know what's your
    opinion.

Lucius. My thoughts, I must confess, are
    turn'd on peace.
Already have our quarrels fill'd the world
With widows, and with orphans: Scythia
    mourns
Our guilty wars, and earth's remotest regions
Lie half unpeopled by the feuds of Rome:
'Tis time to sheathe the sword, and spare
    mankind.
Already have we shown our love to Rome,
Now let us show submission to the gods.
We took up arms, not to revenge ourselves,
But free the commonwealth; when this end
    fails,
Arms have no further use. Our country's
    cause,
That drew our swords, now wrests them
    from our hands.
And bids us not delight in Roman blood,
Unprofitably shed. What men could do,
Is done already: Heav'n and earth will
    witness,
If Rome must fall, that we are innocent.

Cato. Let us appear nor rash nor diffident;
Immod'rate valour swells into a fault;
And fear, admitted into public councils,
Betrays like treason. Let us shun them both.

Fathers, I cannot see that our affairs
Are grown thus desp'rate: we have bulwarks
    round us;
Within our walls are troops inured to toil
In Afric's heat, and season'd to the sun;
Numidia's spacious kingdom lies behind us,
Ready to rise at its young prince's call.
While there is hope, do not distrust the gods;
But wait, at least, till Cæsar's near approach
Force us to yield. 'Twill never be too late
To sue for chains, and own a conqueror.
Why should Rome fall a moment ere her
    time?
No, let us draw her term of freedom out
In its full length, and spin it to the last,
So shall we gain still one day's liberty;
And let me perish, but in Cato's judgment,
A day, an hour, of virtuous liberty,
Is worth a whole eternity in bondage.

Enter Marcus.

Marcus. Fathers, this moment, as I watch'd
    the gate,
Lodged on my post, a herald is arrived
From Cæsar's camp, and with him comes old
    Decius,
The Roman knight; he carries in his looks
Impatience, and demands to speak with
    Cato.

Cato. By your permission, fathers—bid him
    enter.

[*Exit* Marcus.

Decius was once my friend, but other
    prospects
Have loosed those ties, and bound him fast
    to Cæsar.
His message may determine our resolves.

Enter Decius.

Decius. Cæsar sends health to Cato—

Cato. Could he send it
To Cato's slaughter'd friends, it would be
    welcome.
Are not your orders to address the senate?

Decius. My business is with Cato. Cæsar sees
The straits to which you're driven; and, as he
    knows
Cato's high worth, is anxious for your life.

Cato. My life is grafted on the fate of Rome.
Would he save Cato, bid him spare his
    country.
Tell your dictator this; and tell him, Cato
Disdains a life which he has power to offer.

Decius. Rome and her senators submit to
    Cæsar;
Her gen'rals and her consuls are no more,
Who check'd his conquests, and denied his
    triumphs.
Why will not Cato be this Cæsar's friend?

Cato. These very reasons thou hast urged
    forbid it.

Decius. Cato, I've orders to expostulate
And reason with you, as from friend to
    friend:
Think on the storm that gathers o'er your
    head,
And threatens ev'ry hour to burst upon it;
Still may you stand high in your country's
    honours—
Do but comply, and make your peace with
    Cæsar;
Rome will rejoice, and cast its eyes on Cato,
As on the second of mankind.

Cato. No more;
I must not think of life on such conditions.

Decius. Cæsar is well acquainted with your
    virtues,
And therefore sets this value on your life.
Let him but know the price of Cato's
    friendship,
And name your terms.

Cato. Bid him disband his legions,
Restore the commonwealth to liberty,
Submit his actions to the public censure,
And stand the judgment of a Roman
    senate.
Bid him do this, and Cato is his friend.

Decius. Cato, the world talks loudly of your
    wisdom——

Cato. Nay, more, though Cato's voice was
    ne'er employ'd
To clear the guilty, and to varnish crimes,
Myself will mount the rostrum in his favour,
And strive to gain his pardon from the
    people.

Decius. A style like this becomes a
    conqueror.

Cato. Decius, a style like this becomes a
    Roman.

Decius. What is a Roman, that is Cæsar's foe?

Cato. Greater than Cæsar: he's a friend to
    virtue.

Decius. Consider, Cato, you're in Utica,
And at the head of your own little senate:
You do not thunder in the capitol,
With all the mouths of Rome to second you.

Cato. Let him consider that, who drives us
    hither.
'Tis Cæsar's sword has made Rome's senate
    little,
And thinn'd its ranks. Alas! thy dazzled eye
Beholds this man in a false glaring light,
Which conquest and success have thrown
    upon him;

Did'st thou but view him right, thou'dst see
    him black
With murder, treason, sacrilege, and crimes
That strike my soul with horror but to name
    them.
I know thou look'st on me as on a wretch
Beset with ills, and cover'd with misfortunes;
But, by the gods I swear, millions of worlds
Should never buy me to be like that Cæsar.

Decius. Does Cato send this answer back to
    Cæsar,
For all his gen'rous cares and proffer'd
    friendship?

Cato. His cares for me are insolent and vain:
Presumptuous man! the gods take care of
    Cato.
Would Cæsar show the greatness of his soul,
Bid him employ his care for these my
    friends,
And make good use of his ill-gotten pow'r,
By sheltering men much better than himself.

Decius. Your high, unconquer'd heart makes
    you forget
You are a man. You rush on your destruction.
But I have done. When I relate hereafter
The tale of this unhappy embassy,
All Rome will be in tears.[*Exit* Decius.

Sempronius. Cato, we thank thee.
The mighty genius of immortal Rome
Speaks in thy voice; thy soul breathes liberty.

Cæsar will shrink to hear the words thou
    utter'st,
And shudder in the midst of all his
    conquests.

Lucius. The senate owns its gratitude to Cato,
Who with so great a soul consults its safety,
And guards our lives, while he neglects
    his own.

Sempronius. Sempronius gives no thanks on
    this account.
Lucius seems fond of life; but what is life?
'Tis not to stalk about, and draw fresh air
From time to time, or gaze upon the sun;
'Tis to be free. When liberty is gone,
Life grows insipid.

Cato. Come; no more, Sempronius;
All here are friends to Rome, and to each
    other.
Let us not weaken still the weaker side
By our divisions.

Sempronius. Cato, my resentments
Are sacrificed to Rome—I stand reproved.

Cato. Fathers, 'tis time you come to a
    resolve.

Lucius. Cato, we all go in to your opinion;
Cæsar's behaviour has convinced the senate
We ought to hold it out till terms arrive.

Sempronius. We ought to hold it out till
　　death; but, Cato,
My private voice is drown'd amidst the
　　senate's.

Cato. Then let us rise, my friends, and strive
　　to fill
This little interval, this pause of life
(While yet our liberty and fates are doubtful)
With resolution, friendship, Roman bravery,
And all the virtues we can crowd into it;
That Heav'n may say, it ought to be
　　prolong'd.
Fathers, farewell—The young Numidian
　　prince
Comes forward, and expects to know our
　　counsels.

　　　　　　　　　　　　[*Exeunt* Senators.

Enter Juba.

Juba, the Roman senate has resolved,
Till time give better prospects, still to keep
The sword unsheathed, and turn its edge on
　　Cæsar.

Juba. The resolution fits a Roman senate.
But, Cato, lend me for a while thy patience,
And condescend to hear a young man speak.
My father, when, some days before his death,
He order'd me to march for Utica,
(Alas! I thought not then his death so near!)
Wept o'er me, press'd me in his aged arms,

And, as his griefs gave way, "My son," said he,
"Whatever fortune shall befal thy father,
Be Cato's friend; he'll train thee up to great
And virtuous deeds; do but observe him
          well,
Thou'lt shun misfortunes, or thou'lt learn to
          bear them."

Cato. Juba, thy father was a worthy prince,
And merited, alas! a better fate;
But Heav'n thought otherwise.

Juba. My father's fate,
In spite of all the fortitude that shines
Before my face, in Cato's great example,
Subdues my soul, and fills my eyes with
          tears.

Cato. It is an honest sorrow, and becomes
          thee.

Juba. My father drew respect from foreign
          climes:
The kings of Afric sought him for their
          friend;
Kings far remote, that rule, as fame reports,
Behind the hidden sources of the Nile,
In distant worlds, on t'other side the sun;
Oft have their black ambassadors appear'd,
Loaden with gifts, and fill'd the courts of
          Zama.

Cato. I am no stranger to thy father's
          greatness.

Juba. I would not boast the greatness of my
        father,
But point out new alliances to Cato.
Had we not better leave this Utica,
To arm Numidia in our cause, and court
Th' assistance of my father's powerful
        friends?
Did they know Cato, our remotest kings
Would pour embattled multitudes
        about him:
Their swarthy hosts would darken all our
        plains,
Doubling the native horror of the war,
And making death more grim.

Cato. And canst thou think
Cato will fly before the sword of Cæsar?
Reduced, like Hannibal, to seek relief
From court to court, and wander up
        and down
A vagabond in Afric?

Juba. Cato, perhaps
I'm too officious; but my forward cares
Would fain preserve a life of so much value.
My heart is wounded, when I see such virtue
Afflicted by the weight of such misfortunes.

Cato. Thy nobleness of soul obliges me.
But know, young prince, that valour soars
        above
What the world calls misfortune and
        affliction.

These are not ills; else would they never fall
On Heav'n's first fav'rites, and the best
    of men.
The gods, in bounty, work up storms
    about us,
That give mankind occasion to exert
Their hidden strength, and throw out into
    practice
Virtues, which shun the day, and lie
    conceal'd
In the smooth seasons and the calms of life.

Juba. I'm charm'd, whene'er thou talk'st; I
    pant for virtue,
And all my soul endeavours at perfection.

Cato. Dost thou love watchings, abstinence,
    and toil,
Laborious virtues all? Learn them from Cato;
Success and fortune must thou learn from
    Cæsar.

Juba. The best good fortune that can fall on
    Juba,
The whole success at which my heart
    aspires,
Depends on Cato.

Cato. What does Juba say?
Thy words confound me.

Juba. I would fain retract them.
Give them me back again: they aimed at
    nothing.

Cato. Tell me thy wish, young prince; make
    not my ear
A stranger to thy thoughts.

Juba. Oh! they're extravagant;
Still let me hide them.

Cato. What can Juba ask,
That Cato will refuse?

Juba. I fear to name it.
Marcia—inherits all her father's virtues.

Cato. What wouldst thou say?

Juba. Cato, thou hast a daughter.

Cato. Adieu, young prince; I would not hear
    a word
Should lessen thee in my esteem.
    Remember,
The hand of fate is over us, and Heav'n
Exacts severity from all our thoughts.
It is not now a time to talk of aught
But chains or conquest, liberty or death.[*Exit.*

Enter Syphax.

Syphax. How's this, my prince? What, cover'd
    with confusion?
You look as if yon stern philosopher
Had just now chid you.

Juba. Syphax, I'm undone!

Syphax. I know it well.

Juba. Cato thinks meanly of me.

Syphax. And so will all mankind.

Juba. I've open'd to him
The weakness of my soul—my love for
    Marcia.

Syphax. Cato's a proper person to intrust
A love-tale with!

Juba. Oh, I could pierce my heart,
My foolish heart!

Syphax. Alas, my prince, how are you
    changed of late!
I've known young Juba rise before the sun,
To beat the thicket where the tiger slept,
Or seek the lion in his dreadful haunts.
I've seen you,
Ev'n in the Lybian dog-days, hunt him down,
Then charge him close,
And, stooping from your horse,
Rivet the panting savage to the ground.

Juba. Pr'ythee, no more.

Syphax. How would the old king smile,
To see you weigh the paws, when tipp'd with
    gold,

And throw the shaggy spoils about your
    shoulders!

Juba. Syphax, this old man's talk, though
    honey flow'd
In ev'ry word, would now lose all its
    sweetness.
Cato's displeased, and Marcia lost for ever.

Syphax. Young prince, I yet could give you
    good advice;
Marcia might still be yours.

Juba. As how, dear Syphax?

Syphax. Juba commands Numidia's hardy
    troops,
Mounted on steeds unused to the restraint
Of curbs or bits, and fleeter than the winds:
Give but the word, we snatch this damsel up,
And bear her off.

Juba. Can such dishonest thoughts
Rise up in man? Wouldst thou seduce my
    youth
To do an act that would destroy mine
    honour?

Syphax. Gods, I could tear my hair to hear
    you talk!
Honour's a fine imaginary notion,
That draws in raw and inexperienced men
To real mischiefs, while they hunt a shadow.

Juba. Wouldst thou degrade thy prince into a
    ruffian?

Syphax. The boasted ancestors of these
    great men,
Whose virtues you admire, were all such
    ruffians.
This dread of nations, this almighty Rome,
That comprehends in her wide empire's
    bounds
All under Heav'n, was founded on a rape;
Your Scipios, Cæsars, Pompeys, and your
    Catos
(The gods on earth), are all the spurious
    blood
Of violated maids, of ravish'd Sabines.

Juba. Syphax, I fear that hoary head of thine
Abounds too much in our Numidian wiles.

Syphax. Indeed, my prince, you want to
    know the world.

Juba. If knowledge of the world makes men
    perfidious,
May Juba ever live in ignorance!

Syphax. Go, go; you're young.

Juba. Gods, must I tamely bear
This arrogance, unanswer'd! Thou'rt a
    traitor,
A false old traitor.

Syphax. I've gone too far.[*Aside.*

Juba. Cato shall know the baseness of thy
      soul.

Syphax. I must appease this storm, or perish
      in it. [*Aside.*
Young prince, behold these locks, that are
      grown white
Beneath a helmet in your father's battles.

Juba. Those locks shall ne'er protect thy
      insolence.

Syphax. Must one rash word, the infirmity
      of age,
Throw down the merit of my better years?
This the reward of a whole life of service!—
Curse on the boy! how steadily he hears me!
      [*Aside.*

Juba. Syphax, no more! I would not hear you
      talk.

Syphax. Not hear me talk! what, when my
      faith to Juba,
My royal master's son, is call'd in question?
My prince may strike me dead, and I'll be
      dumb;
But whilst I live I must not hold my tongue,
And languish out old age in his displeasure.

Juba. Thou know'st the way too well into my
      heart.

I do believe thee loyal to thy prince.

Syphax. What greater instance can I give?
    I've offer'd
To do an action which my soul abhors,
And gain you whom you love, at any price.

Juba. Was this thy motive? I have been too
    hasty.

Syphax. And 'tis for this my prince has call'd
    me traitor.

Juba. Sure thou mistakest; I did not call
    thee so.

Syphax. You did, indeed, my prince, you
    call'd me traitor.
Nay, further, threatened you'd complain to
    Cato.
Of what, my prince, would you complain to
    Cato?
That Syphax loves you, and would sacrifice
His life, nay, more, his honour, in your
    service?

Juba. Syphax, I know thou lovest me; but
    indeed
Thy zeal for Juba carried thee too far.
Honour's a sacred tie, the law of kings,
The noble mind's distinguishing perfection,
That aids and strengthens Virtue where it
    meets her,
And imitates her actions where she is not;

It ought not to be sported with.

Syphax. Believe me, prince, you make old
    Syphax weep
To hear you talk—but 'tis with tears of joy.
If e'er your father's crown adorn your brows,
Numidia will be blest by Cato's lectures.

Juba. Syphax, thy hand; we'll mutually forget
The warmth of youth, and forwardness
    of age:
Thy prince esteems thy worth, and loves thy
    person.
If e'er the sceptre come into my hand,
Syphax shall stand the second in my
    kingdom.

Syphax. Why will you overwhelm my age
    with kindness?
My joys grow burdensome, I sha'n't
    support it.

Juba. Syphax, farewell. I'll hence, and try
    to find
Some blest occasion, that may set me right
In Cato's thoughts. I'd rather have that man
Approve my deeds, than worlds for my
    admirers.[*Exit.*

Syphax. Young men soon give, and soon
    forget, affronts;
Old age is slow in both—A false old traitor!
These words, rash boy, may chance to cost
    thee dear.

My heart had still some foolish fondness for
    thee;
But hence, 'tis gone! I give it to the winds:
Cæsar, I'm wholly thine.

Enter Sempronius.

All hail, Sempronius!
Well, Cato's senate is resolved to wait
The fury of a siege, before it yields.

Sempronius. Syphax, we both were on the
    verge of fate;
Lucius declared for peace, and terms were
    offer'd
To Cato, by a messenger from Cæsar.
Should they submit, ere our designs are ripe,
We both must perish in the common wreck,
Lost in the general, undistinguish'd ruin.

Syphax. But how stands Cato?

Sempronius. Thou hast seen mount Atlas:
Whilst storms and tempests thunder on its
    brows,
And oceans break their billows at its feet,
It stands unmoved, and glories in its height;
Such is that haughty man; his tow'ring soul,
'Midst all the shocks and injuries of fortune,
Rises superior, and looks down on Cæsar.

Syphax. But what's this messenger?

Sempronius. I've practised with him,

And found a means to let the victor know
That Syphax and Sempronius are his
    friends.
But let me now examine in my turn;
Is Juba fix'd?

Syphax. Yes—but it is to Cato.
I've tried the force of every reason on him,
Soothed and caress'd; been angry, soothed
    again;
Laid safety, life, and interest in his sight;
But all are vain, he scorns them all for Cato.

Sempronius. Come, 'tis no matter; we shall do
    without him.
He'll make a pretty figure in a triumph,
And serve to trip before the victor's chariot.
Syphax, I now may hope thou hast forsook
Thy Juba's cause, and wishest Marcia mine.

Syphax. May she be thine as fast as thou
    wouldst have her.

Sempronius. Syphax, I love that woman;
    though I curse
Her and myself, yet, spite of me, I love her.

Syphax. Make Cato sure, and give up Utica,
Cæsar will ne'er refuse thee such a trifle.
But are thy troops prepared for a revolt?
Does the sedition catch from man to man,
And run among the ranks?

Sempronius. All, all is ready;

The factious leaders are our friends, that
    spread
Murmurs and discontents among the
    soldiers;
They count their toilsome marches, long
    fatigues,
Unusual fastings, and will hear no more
This medley of philosophy and war.
Within an hour they'll storm the senate
    house.

Syphax. Meanwhile I'll draw up my
    Numidian troops
Within the square, to exercise their arms,
And, as I see occasion, favour thee.
I laugh, to see how your unshaken Cato
Will look aghast, while unforeseen
    destruction
Pours in upon him thus from every side.
So, where our wide Numidian wastes extend,
Sudden th' impetuous hurricanes descend,
Wheel through the air, in circling eddies
    play,
Tear up the sands, and sweep whole plains
    away.
The helpless traveller, with wild surprise,
Sees the dry desert all around him rise,
And, smother'd in the dusty whirlwind, dies.
    [*Exeunt.*

ACT THE THIRD

SCENE I.
A Chamber.
Enter Marcus *and* Portius.

Marcus. Thanks to my stars, I have not ranged about
The wilds of life, ere I could find a friend;
Nature first pointed out my Portius to me,
And early taught me, by her secret force,
To love thy person, ere I knew thy merit,
Till what was instinct, grew up into friendship.

Portius. Marcus, the friendships of the world are oft
Confed'racies in vice, or leagues of pleasure;
Ours has severest virtue for its basis,
And such a friendship ends not but with life.

Marcus. Portius, thou know'st my soul in all its weakness;
Then, pr'ythee, spare me on its tender side;

Indulge me but in love, my other passions
Shall rise and fall by virtue's nicest rules.

Portius. When love's well-timed, 'tis not a
          fault to love.
The strong, the brave, the virtuous, and the
          wise,
Sink in the soft captivity together.

Marcus. Alas, thou talk'st like one that
          never felt
Th' impatient throbs and longings of a soul,
That pants and reaches after distant good!
A lover does not live by vulgar time;
Believe me, Portius, in my Lucia's absence
Life hangs upon me, and becomes a burden;
And yet, when I behold the charming maid,
I'm ten times more undone; while hope and
          fear,
And grief and rage, and love, rise up at
          once,
And with variety of pain distract me.

Portius. What can thy Portius do to give thee
          help?

Marcus. Portius, thou oft enjoy'st the fair
          one's presence;
Then undertake my cause, and plead it
          to her
With all the strength and heat of eloquence
Fraternal love and friendship can inspire.
Tell her thy brother languishes to death,
And fades away, and withers in his bloom;

That he forgets his sleep, and loathes his
    food;
That youth, and health, and war, are joyless
    to him;
Describe his anxious days, and restless
    nights,
And all the torments that thou see'st me
    suffer.

Portius. Marcus, I beg thee give me not an
    office,
That suits with me so ill. Thou know'st my
    temper.

Marcus. Wilt thou behold me sinking in my
    woes,
And wilt thou not reach out a friendly arm,
To raise me from amidst this plunge of
    sorrows?

Portius. Marcus, thou canst not ask what I'd
    refuse;
But here, believe me, I've a thousand
    reasons——

Marcus. I know thou'lt say my passion's out
    of season,
That Cato's great example and misfortunes
Should both conspire to drive it from my
    thoughts.
But what's all this to one that loves like me?
O Portius, Portius, from my soul I wish
Thou did'st but know thyself what 'tis to
    love!

Then wouldst thou pity and assist thy
    brother.

Portius. What should I do? If I disclose my
    passion,
Our friendship's at an end: if I conceal it,
The world will call me false to a friend and
    brother.[*Aside.*

Marcus. But see, where Lucia, at her wonted
    hour,
Amid the cool of yon high marble arch,
Enjoys the noon-day breeze! Observe her,
    Portius;
That face, that shape, those eyes, that heav'n
    of beauty!
Observe her well, and blame me if thou
    canst.

Portius. She sees us, and advances——

Marcus. I'll withdraw,
And leave you for a while. Remember,
    Portius,
Thy brother's life depends upon thy tongue.
    [*Exit.*

Enter Lucia.

Lucia. Did not I see your brother Marcus
    here?
Why did he fly the place, and shun my
    presence?

Portius. Oh, Lucia, language is too faint
    to show
His rage of love; it preys upon his life;
He pines, he sickens, he despairs, he dies!

Lucia. How wilt thou guard thy honour, in
    the shock
Of love and friendship! Think betimes, my
    Portius,
Think how the nuptial tie, that might ensure
Our mutual bliss, would raise to such a
    height
Thy brother's griefs, as might perhaps
    destroy him.

Portius. Alas, poor youth! What dost thou
    think, my Lucia?
His gen'rous, open, undesigning heart
Has begg'd his rival to solicit for him!
Then do not strike him dead with a denial.

Lucia. No, Portius, no; I see thy sister's tears,
Thy father's anguish, and thy brother's
    death,
In the pursuit of our ill-fated loves;
And, Portius, here I swear, to Heav'n I swear,
To Heav'n, and all the powers that judge
    mankind,
Never to mix my plighted hands with thine,
While such a cloud of mischief hangs
    upon us,
But to forget our loves, and drive thee out
From all my thoughts—as far as I am able.

Portius. What hast thou said? I'm
    thunderstruck—recall
Those hasty words, or I am lost for ever.

Lucia. Has not the vow already pass'd my
    lips?
The gods have heard it, and 'tis seal'd in
    heav'n.
May all the vengeance that was ever pour'd
On perjured heads, o'erwhelm me if I
    break it!

Portius. Fix'd in astonishment, I gaze upon
    thee,
Like one just blasted by a stroke from heav'n,
Who pants for breath and stiffens, yet alive,
In dreadful looks, a monument of wrath!

Lucia. Think, Portius, think thou see'st thy
    dying brother
Stabb'd at his heart, and all besmear'd with
    blood,
Storming at Heav'n and thee! Thy awful sire
Sternly demands the cause, the accursed
    cause,
That robs him of his son: poor Marcia
    trembles,
Then tears her hair, and, frantic in her
    griefs,
Calls out on Lucia. What could Lucia
    answer,
Or how stand up in such a scene of sorrow?

Portius. To my confusion and eternal grief,

I must approve the sentence that destroys
    me.

Lucia. Portius, no more; thy words shoot
    through my heart,
Melt my resolves, and turn me all to love.
Why are those tears of fondness in thy eyes?
Why heaves thy heart? Why swells thy soul
    with sorrow?
It softens me too much—Farewell, my
    Portius!
Farewell, though death is in the word,—for
    ever!

Portius. Stay, Lucia, stay! What dost thou say?
    For ever?
Thou must not go; my soul still hovers o'er
    thee,
And can't get loose.

Lucia. If the firm Portius shake,
To hear of parting, think what Lucia suffers!

Portius. 'Tis true, unruffled and serene,
    I've met
The common accidents of life, but here
Such an unlook'd-for storm of ills falls
    on me.
It beats down all my strength—I cannot
    bear it.
We must not part.

Lucia. What dost thou say? Not part!
Hast thou forgot the vow that I have made?

Are not there heavens, and gods, that
    thunder o'er us?
—But see, thy brother Marcus bends
    this way;
I sicken at the sight. Once more, farewell.
Farewell, and know, thou wrong'st me, if
    thou think'st
Ever was love or ever grief like mine.[*Exit* Lucia.

Enter Marcus.

Marcus. Portius, what hopes? How stands
    she? am I doom'd
To life or death?

Portius. What wouldst thou have me say?

Marcus. What means this pensive posture?
    Thou appear'st
Like one amazed and terrified.

Portius. I've reason.

Marcus. Thy downcast looks, and thy
    disorder'd thoughts,
Tell me my fate. I ask not the success
My cause has found.

Portius. I'm grieved I undertook it.

Marcus. What, does the barbarous maid
    insult my heart,
My aching heart, and triumph in my pains?

That I could cast her from my thoughts for
    ever!

Portius. Away! you're too suspicious in your
    griefs;
Lucia, though sworn never to think of love,
Compassionates your pains, and pities you.

Marcus. Compassionates my pains, and
    pities me!
What is compassion, when 'tis void of love?
Fool that I was, to choose so cold a friend
To urge my cause!—Compassionates my
    pains!
Pr'ythee what art, what rhet'ric didst
    thou use
To gain this mighty boon?—She pities me!
To one that asks the warm returns of love,
Compassion's cruelty, 'tis scorn, 'tis death—

Portius. Marcus, no more; have I deserved
    this treatment?

Marcus. What have I said? Oh! Portius, Oh,
    forgive me!
A soul exasperated in ills, falls out
With every thing—its friend, itself—but hah!
    [*Shout.*
What means that shout, big with the sounds
    of war?
What new alarm?

Portius. A second, louder yet,

Swells in the wind, and comes more full
    upon us.

Marcus. Oh, for some glorious cause to fall in
    battle!
Lucia, thou hast undone me: thy disdain
Has broke my heart; 'tis death must give me
    ease.

Portius. Quick let us hence. Who knows if
    Cato's life
Stands sure? Oh, Marcus, I am warm'd; my
    heart
Leaps at the trumpet's voice, and burns for
    glory.[*Exeunt.*

Scene II.
Part of the Senate House.
Enter Sempronius, *with* Leaders *of the Mutiny.*

Sempronius. At length the winds are raised,
    the storm blows high!
Be it your care, my friends, to keep it up
In all its fury, and direct it right,
Till it has spent itself on Cato's head.
Meanwhile, I'll herd among his friends,
    and seem
One of the number, that, whate'er arrive,
My friends and fellow soldiers may be safe.
    [*Exit.*

1 Lead. We are all safe; Sempronius is our
    friend.
Sempronius is as brave a man as Cato.

But, hark, he enters. Bear up boldly to him;
Be sure you beat him down, and bind him
    fast;
This day will end our toils.
Fear nothing, for Sempronius is our friend.

    Enter Sempronius, *with* Cato, Lucius,
        Portius, *and* Marcus.

Cato. Where are those bold, intrepid sons
    of war,
That greatly turn their backs upon the foe,
And to their general send a brave defiance?

Sempronius. Curse on their dastard souls,
    they stand astonish'd!

                [*Aside.*

Cato. Perfidious men! And will you thus
    dishonour
Your past exploits, and sully all your wars?
Why could not Cato fall
Without your guilt! Behold, ungrateful men,
Behold my bosom naked to your swords,
And let the man that's injured strike the
    blow.
Which of you all suspects that he is
    wrong'd,
Or thinks he suffers greater ills than Cato?
Am I distinguished from you but by toils,
Superior toils, and heavier weight of cares?
Painful pre-eminence!

Sempronius. Confusion to the villains! all is
    lost![*Aside.*

Cato. Have you forgotten Lybia's burning
    waste,
Its barren rocks, parch'd earth, and hills of
    sand,
Its tainted air, and all its broods of poison?
Who was the first to explore th' untrodden
    path,
When life was hazarded in ev'ry step?
Or, fainting in the long laborious march,
When, on the banks of an unlook'd-for
    stream,
You sunk the river with repeated draughts,
Who was the last of all your host who
    thirsted?

Sempronius. Did not his temples glow
In the same sultry winds and scorching
    heats?

Cato. Hence, worthless men! hence! and
    complain to Cæsar,
You could not undergo the toil of war,
Nor bear the hardships that your leader
    bore.

Lucius. See, Cato, see the unhappy men: they
    weep!
Fear, and remorse, and sorrow for their
    crime,
Appear in ev'ry look, and plead for mercy.

Cato. Learn to be honest men; give up yon
    leaders,
And pardon shall descend on all the rest.

Sempronius. Cato, commit these wretches to
    my care;
First let them each be broken on the rack,
Then, with what life remains, impaled,
    and left
To writhe at leisure round the bloody stake;
There let them hang, and taint the southern
    wind.
The partners of their crime will learn
    obedience.

Cato. Forbear, Sempronius!—see they suffer
    death,
But in their deaths remember they are men;
Strain not the laws, to make their tortures
    grievous.
Lucius, the base, degen'rate age requires
Severity.
When by just vengeance guilty mortals
    perish,
The gods behold the punishment with
    pleasure,
And lay th' uplifted thunderbolt aside.

Sempronius. Cato, I execute thy will with
    pleasure.

Cato. Meanwhile, we'll sacrifice to liberty.
Remember, O my friends! the laws, the
    rights,

The gen'rous plan of power delivered down
From age to age by your renown'd
    forefathers,
(So dearly bought, the price of so much
    blood:)
Oh, let it never perish in your hands!
But piously transmit it to your children.
Do thou, great liberty, inspire our souls,
And make our lives in thy possession happy,
Or our deaths glorious in thy just defence.

[*Exeunt* Cato, *etc.*

1 Lead. Sempronius, you have acted like
    yourself.
One would have thought you had been half
    in earnest.

Sempronius. Villain, stand off; base, grov'ling,
    worthless wretches,
Mongrels in faction, poor faint-hearted
    traitors!

1 Lead. Nay, now, you carry it too far,
    Sempronius!

Sempronius. Know, villains, when such paltry
    slaves presume
To mix in treason, if the plot succeeds,
They're thrown neglected by; but if it fails,
They're sure to die like dogs, as you shall do.
Here, take these factious monsters, drag
    them forth
To sudden death.

1 Lead. Nay, since it comes to this—

Sempronius. Dispatch them quick, but first
    pluck out their tongues,
Lest with their dying breath they sow
    sedition.

[*Exeunt* Guards, *with their* Leaders.

Enter Syphax.

Syphax. Our first design, my friend, has
    proved abortive;
Still there remains an after-game to play;
My troops are mounted;
Let but Sempronius head us in our flight,
We'll force the gate where Marcus keeps his
    guard,
And hew down all that would oppose our
    passage.
A day will bring us into Cæsar's camp.

Sempronius. Confusion! I have fail'd of half
    my purpose:
Marcia, the charming Marcia's left behind!

Syphax. How! will Sempronius turn a
    woman's slave?

Sempronius. Think not thy friend can ever
    feel the soft
Unmanly warmth and tenderness of love.
Syphax, I long to clasp that haughty maid,

And bend her stubborn virtue to my passion:
When I have gone thus far, I'd cast her off.

Syphax. Well said! that's spoken like thyself,
    Sempronius!
What hinders, then, but that thou find
    her out,
And hurry her away by manly force?

Sempronius. But how to gain admission? For
    access
Is given to none but Juba, and her brothers.

Syphax. Thou shalt have Juba's dress, and
    Juba's guards;
The doors will open, when Numidia's prince
Seems to appear before the slaves that watch
    them.

Sempronius. Heavens, what a thought is
    there! Marcia's my own!
How will my bosom swell with anxious joy,
When I behold her struggling in my arms,
With glowing beauty, and disorder'd charms,
While fear and anger, with alternate grace,
Pant in her breast, and vary in her face!
So Pluto seized off Proserpine, convey'd
To hell's tremendous gloom th' affrighted
    maid;
There grimly smiled, pleased with the
    beauteous prize,
Nor envied Jove his sunshine and his skies.
    [*Exeunt.*

ACT THE FOURTH

Scene I.
A Chamber.
Enter Lucia *and* Marcia.

Lucia. Now, tell me, Marcia, tell me from thy
    soul,
If thou believest 'tis possible for woman
To suffer greater ills than Lucia suffers?

Marcia. Oh, Lucia, Lucia, might my big
    swol'n heart
Vent all its griefs, and give a loose to sorrow,
Marcia could answer thee in sighs, keep pace
With all thy woes, and count out tear for tear.

Lucia. I know thou'rt doom'd alike to be
    beloved
By Juba, and thy father's friend, Sempronius:
But which of these has power to charm like
    Portius?

Marcia. Still, I must beg thee not to name
     Sempronius.
Lucia, I like not that loud, boist'rous man.
Juba, to all the bravery of a hero,
Adds softest love, and more than female
     sweetness;
Juba might make the proudest of our sex,
Any of womankind, but Marcia, happy.

Lucia. And why not Marcia? Come, you strive
     in vain
To hide your thoughts from one who knows
     too well
The inward glowings of a heart in love.

Marcia. While Cato lives, his daughter has no
     right
To love or hate, but as his choice directs.

Lucia. But should this father give you to
     Sempronius?

Marcia. I dare not think he will: but if he
     should—
Why wilt thou add to all the griefs I suffer,
Imaginary ills, and fancied tortures?
I hear the sound of feet! They march
     this way.
Let us retire, and try if we can drown
Each softer thought in sense of present
     danger:
When love once pleads admission to our
     hearts,
In spite of all the virtues we can boast,

The woman that deliberates is lost.[*Exeunt.*

Enter Sempronius, *dressed like* Juba, *with* Numidian
Guards.

Sempronius. The deer is lodged, I've track'd
her to her covert.
How will the young Numidian rave to see
His mistress lost! If aught could glad my soul,
Beyond the enjoyment of so bright a prize,
'Twould be to torture that young, gay
barbarian.
—But, hark! what noise! Death to my hopes!
'tis he,
'Tis Juba's self! there is but one way left——

Enter Juba.

Juba. What do I see? Who's this that dares
usurp
The guards and habits of Numidia's prince?

Sempronius. One that was born to scourge
thy arrogance,
Presumptuous youth!

Juba. What can this mean? Sempronius!

Sempronius. My sword shall answer thee.
Have at thy heart.

Juba. Nay then, beware thy own, proud,
barbarous man.

[Sempronius *falls.*

Sempronius. Curse on my stars! Am I then
    doom'd to fall
By a boy's hand, disfigured in a vile
Numidian dress, and for a worthless woman?
Gods, I'm distracted! this my close of life!
Oh, for a peal of thunder, that would make
Earth, sea, and air, and heav'n, and Cato
    tremble![*Dies.*

Juba. I'll hence to Cato,
That we may there at length unravel all
This dark design, this mystery of fate.
    [*Exit* Juba.

      Enter Lucia *and* Marcia.

Lucia. Sure 'twas the clash of swords; my
    troubled heart
Is so cast down, and sunk amidst its sorrows,
It throbs with fear, and aches at ev'ry sound.
Oh, Marcia, should thy brothers, for my
    sake—
I die away with horror at the thought!

Marcia. See, Lucia, see! here's blood! here's
    blood and murder!
Ha! a Numidian! Heav'n preserve the prince!
The face lies muffled up within the garment,
But ah! death to my sight! a diadem,
And royal robes! O gods! 'tis he, 'tis he!
Juba lies dead before us!

Lucia. Now, Marcia, now, call up to thy
    assistance
Thy wonted strength and constancy of mind;
Thou canst not put it to a greater trial.

Marcia. Lucia, look there, and wonder at my
    patience;
Have I not cause to rave, and beat my breast,
To rend my heart with grief, and run
    distracted?

Lucia. What can I think, or say, to give thee
    comfort?

Marcia. Talk not of comfort, 'tis for lighter
    ills:
Behold a sight that strikes all comfort dead.

Enter Juba, *listening.*

I will indulge my sorrows, and give way
To all the pangs and fury of despair;
That man, that best of men, deserved it
    from me.

Juba. What do I hear? and was the false
    Sempronius
That best of men? Oh, had I fall'n like him,
And could have been thus mourn'd, I had
    been happy.

Marcia. 'Tis not in fate to ease my tortured
    breast.
Oh, he was all made up of love and charms!

Whatever maid could wish, or man admire:
Delight of every eye; when he appear'd,
A secret pleasure gladden'd all that saw him;
But when he talk'd, the proudest Roman
    blush'd
To hear his virtues, and old age grew wise.
Oh, Juba! Juba!

Juba. What means that voice? Did she not
    call on Juba?

Marcia. Why do I think on what he was? he's
    dead!
He's dead, and never knew how much I
    loved him!
Lucia, who knows but his poor, bleeding
    heart,
Amidst its agonies, remember'd Marcia,
And the last words he utter'd call'd me cruel!
Alas! he knew not, hapless youth, he
    knew not
Marcia's whole soul was full of love and Juba!

Juba. Where am I? Do I live? or am indeed
What Marcia thinks? All is Elysium
    round me!

Marcia. Ye dear remains of the most loved
    of men,
Nor modesty nor virtue here forbid
A last embrace, while thus——

Juba. See, Marcia, see,[*Throwing himself
before her.*

The happy Juba lives! he lives to catch
That dear embrace, and to return it too,
With mutual warmth, and eagerness of love.

Marcia. With pleasure and amaze I stand
    transported!
If thou art Juba, who lies there?

Juba. A wretch,
Disguised like Juba on a cursed design.
I could not bear
To leave thee in the neighbourhood of death,
But flew, in all the haste of love, to find thee;
I found thee weeping, and confess this once,
Am rapt with joy, to see my Marcia's tears.

Marcia. I've been surprised in an unguarded
    hour,
But must not go back; the love, that lay
Half smother'd in my breast, has broke
    through all
Its weak restraints, and burns in its full
    lustre.
I cannot, if I would, conceal it from thee.

Juba. My joy, my best beloved, my only wish!
How shall I speak the transport of my soul!

Marcia. Lucia, thy arm. Lead to my
    apartment.
Oh! prince! I blush to think what I have said,
But fate has wrested the confession from me;
Go on, and prosper in the paths of honour.
Thy virtue will excuse my passion for thee,

And make the gods propitious to our love.

　　　　　　　　　　[*Exeunt* Marcia *and* Lucia.

Juba. I am so blest, I fear 'tis all a dream.
Fortune, thou now hast made amends for all
Thy past unkindness: I absolve my stars.
What though Numidia add her conquer'd
　　　towns
And provinces to swell the victor's triumph,
Juba will never at his fate repine:
Let Cæsar have the world, if Marcia's mine.
　　　[*Exit.*

SCENE II.
The Stret.
A March at a distance.
Enter Cato *and* Lucius.

Lucius. I stand astonish'd! What, the bold
　　　Sempronius,
That still broke foremost through the crowd
　　　of patriots,
As with a hurricane of zeal transported,
And virtuous even to madness—

Cato. Trust me, Lucius,
Our civil discords have produced such
　　　crimes,
Such monstrous crimes, I am surprized at
　　　nothing.
—Oh Lucius, I am sick of this bad world!
The daylight and the sun grow painful to me.

Enter Portius.

But see, where Portius comes: what means
    this haste?
Why are thy looks thus changed?

Portius. My heart is grieved,
I bring such news as will afflict my father.

Cato. Has Cæsar shed more Roman blood?

Portius. Not so.
The traitor Syphax, as within the square
He exercised his troops, the signal given,
Flew off at once with his Numidian horse
To the south gate, where Marcus holds the
    watch;
I saw, and call'd to stop him, but in vain:
He toss'd his arm aloft, and proudly told me,
He would not stay, and perish, like
    Sempronius.

Cato. Perfidious man! But haste, my son,
    and see
Thy brother Marcus acts a Roman's part.
    [*Exit* Portius.
—Lucius, the torrent bears too hard
    upon me:
Justice gives way to force: the conquer'd
    world
Is Cæsar's! Cato has no business in it.

Lucius. While pride, oppression, and
    injustice reign,

The world will still demand her Cato's
    presence.
In pity to mankind submit to Cæsar,
And reconcile thy mighty soul to life.

Cato. Would Lucius have me live to swell the
    number
Of Cæsar's slaves, or by a base submission
Give up the cause of Rome, and own a
    tyrant?

Lucius. The victor never will impose on Cato
Ungen'rous terms. His enemies confess
The virtues of humanity are Cæsar's.

Cato. Curse on his virtues! they've undone
    his country.
Such popular humanity is treason——
But see young Juba; the good youth
    appears,
Full of the guilt of his perfidious subjects!

Lucius. Alas, poor prince! his fate deserves
    compassion.

Enter Juba.

Juba. I blush, and am confounded to appear
Before thy presence, Cato.

Cato. What's thy crime?

Juba. I'm a Numidian.

Cato. And a brave one, too. Thou hast a
    Roman soul.

Juba. Hast thou not heard of my false
    countrymen?

Cato. Alas, young prince!
Falsehood and fraud shoot up in ev'ry soil,
The product of all climes—Rome has its
    Cæsars.

Juba. 'Tis generous thus to comfort the
    distress'd.

Cato. 'Tis just to give applause, where 'tis
    deserved:
Thy virtue, prince, has stood the test of
    fortune,
Like purest gold, that, tortured in the
    furnace,
Comes out more bright, and brings forth all
    its weight.

Juba. What shall I answer thee?
I'd rather gain
Thy praise, O Cato! than Numidia's empire.

Enter Portius.

Portius. Misfortune on misfortune! grief on
    grief!
My brother Marcus——

Cato. Ha! what has he done?

Has he forsook his post? Has he given way?
Did he look tamely on, and let them pass?

Portius. Scarce had I left my father, but I
    met him
Borne on the shields of his surviving
    soldiers,
Breathless and pale, and cover'd o'er with
    wounds.
Long, at the head of his few faithful friends,
He stood the shock of a whole host of foes,
Till, obstinately brave, and bent on death,
Oppress'd with multitudes, he greatly fell.

Cato. I'm satisfied.

Portius. Nor did he fall, before
His sword had pierced thro' the false heart of
    Syphax.
Yonder he lies. I saw the hoary traitor
Grin in the pangs of death, and bite the
    ground.

Cato. Thanks to the gods, my boy has done
    his duty.
—Portius, when I am dead, be sure you place
His urn near mine.

Portius. Long may they keep asunder!

Lucius. Oh, Cato, arm thy soul with all its
    patience;
See where the corpse of thy dead son
    approaches!

The citizens and senators alarm'd,
Have gather'd round it, and attend it
     weeping.

Cato *meeting the Corpse.*—Senators *attending.*

Cato. Welcome, my son! Here lay him down,
     my friends,
Full in my sight, that I may view at leisure
The bloody corse, and count those glorious
     wounds.
—How beautiful is death, when earn'd by
     virtue!
Who would not be that youth? What pity
     is it,
That we can die but once, to serve our
     country!
—Why sits this sadness on your brows, my
     friends?
I should have blush'd, if Cato's house had
     stood
Secure, and flourish'd in a civil war.
Portius, behold thy brother, and remember,
Thy life is not thy own when Rome
     demands it.

Juba. Was ever man like this!

Cato. Alas, my friends,
Why mourn you thus? let not a private loss
Afflict your hearts. 'Tis Rome requires our
     tears,
The mistress of the world, the seat of empire,
The nurse of heroes, the delight of gods,

That humbled the proud tyrants of the earth,
And set the nations free; Rome is no more.
Oh, liberty! Oh, virtue! Oh, my country!

Juba. Behold that upright man! Rome fills
     his eyes
With tears, that flow'd not o'er his own dear
     son.[*Aside.*

Cato. Whate'er the Roman virtue has
     subdued,
The sun's whole course, the day and year, are
     Cæsar's:
For him the self-devoted Decii died,
The Fabii fell, and the great Scipios
     conquer'd:
Ev'n Pompey fought for Cæsar. Oh, my
     friends,
How is the toil of fate, the work of ages,
The Roman empire, fall'n! Oh, cursed
     ambition!
Fall'n into Cæsar's hands! Our great
     forefathers
Had left him nought to conquer but his
     country.

Juba. While Cato lives, Cæsar will blush
     to see
Mankind enslaved, and be ashamed of
     empire.

Cato. Cæsar ashamed! Has he not seen
     Pharsalia?

Lucius. 'Tis time thou save thyself and us.

Cato. Lose not a thought on me; I'm out of
    danger:
Heaven will not leave me in the victor's hand.
Cæsar shall never say, he conquer'd Cato.
But oh, my friends! your safety fills my heart
With anxious thoughts; a thousand secret
    terrors
Rise in my soul. How shall I save my friends?
'Tis now, O Cæsar, I begin to fear thee!

Lucius. Cæsar has mercy, if we ask it of him.

Cato. Then ask it, I conjure you; let him
    know,
Whate'er was done against him, Cato did it.
Add, if you please, that I request of him,—
That I myself, with tears, request it of him,—
The virtue of my friends may pass
    unpunish'd.
Juba, my heart is troubled for thy sake.
Should I advise thee to regain Numidia,
Or seek the conqueror?

Juba. If I forsake thee
Whilst I have life, may Heaven abandon
    Juba!

Cato. Thy virtues, prince, if I foresee aright,
Will one day make thee great; at Rome,
    hereafter,
'Twill be no crime to have been Cato's
    friend.

Portius, draw near: my son, thou oft
    hast seen
Thy sire engaged in a corrupted state,
Wrestling with vice and faction: now thou
    see'st me
Spent, overpower'd, despairing of success.
Let me advise thee to retreat betimes
To thy paternal seat, the Sabine field;
Where the great Censor toil'd with his own
    hands,
And all our frugal ancestors were bless'd
In humble virtues, and a rural life;
There live retired, pray for the peace of
    Rome;
Content thyself to be obscurely good.
When vice prevails, and impious men bear
    sway,
The post of honour is a private station.

Portius. I hope my father does not
    recommend
A life to Portius that he scorns himself.

Cato. Farewell, my friends! If there be any
    of you
Who dare not trust the victor's clemency,
Know there are ships prepared, by my
    command,
That shall convey you to the wish'd-for port.
Is there aught else, my friends, I can do
    for you?
The conqueror draws near. Once more,
    farewell!
If e'er we meet hereafter, we shall meet

In happier climes, and on a safer shore,
Where Cæsar never shall approach us more.

[*Pointing to his dead son.*

There, the brave youth, with love of virtue
    fired,
Who greatly in his country's cause expired,
Shall know he conquer'd. The firm patriot
    there,
Who made the welfare of mankind his care,
Though still by faction, vice, and fortune
    crost,
Shall find the gen'rous labour was not lost.
    [*Exeunt.*

ACT THE FIFTH

Scene I.

A Chamber.

Cato *solus, sitting in a thoughtful Posture; in his Hand,*
Plato's Book on the Immortality of the Soul.
A drawn Sword on the Table by him.

Cato. It must be so—Plato, thou reason'st
    well—
Else whence this pleasing hope, this fond
    desire,
This longing after immortality?
Or whence this secret dread, and inward
    horror,
Of falling into nought? Why shrinks the soul
Back on herself, and startles at destruction?
'Tis the divinity that stirs within us;
'Tis Heav'n itself that points out an hereafter,
And intimates eternity to man.
Eternity! thou pleasing, dreadful thought!
Through what variety of untried being,
Through what new scenes and changes must
    we pass?

The wide, the unbounded prospect lies
    before me;
But shadows, clouds, and darkness, rest
    upon it.
Here will I hold. If there's a Power above us
(And that there is, all Nature cries aloud
Through all her works), He must delight in
    virtue;
And that which He delights in must be
    happy.
But when, or where?—this world was made
    for Cæsar:
I'm weary of conjectures—this must end
    them.

                [*Laying his hand upon his sword.*

Thus am I doubly arm'd: my death and life,
My bane and antidote, are both before me.
This in a moment brings me to an end;
But this informs me I shall never die.
The soul, secured in her existence, smiles
At the drawn dagger, and defies its point.
The stars shall fade away, the sun himself
Grow dim with age, and nature sink in years,
But thou shalt flourish in immortal youth,
Unhurt amidst the war of elements,
The wreck of matter, and the crush of
    worlds.
What means this heaviness, that hangs
    upon me?
This lethargy, that creeps through all my
    senses?
Nature, oppress'd and harass'd out with care,

Sinks down to rest. This once I'll favour her,
That my awaken'd soul may take her flight,
Renew'd in all her strength, and fresh with
    life,
An offering lit for Heav'n. Let guilt or fear
Disturb man's rest, Cato knows neither of
    them,
Indiff'rent in his choice to sleep or die.

Enter Portius.

But, hah! who's this? my son! Why this
    intrusion?
Were not my orders that I would be private?
Why am I disobey'd?

Portius. Alas, my father!
What means this sword, this instrument of
    death?
Let me convey it hence.

Cato. Rash youth, forbear!

Portius. Oh, let the pray'rs, th' entreaties of
    your friends,
Their tears, their common danger, wrest it
    from you!

Cato. Wouldst thou betray me? Wouldst thou
    give me up,
A slave, a captive, into Cæsar's hands?
Retire, and learn obedience to a father,
Or know, young man—

Portius. Look not thus sternly on me;
You know, I'd rather die than disobey you.

Cato. 'Tis well! again I'm master of myself.
Now, Cæsar, let thy troops beset our gates,
And bar each avenue; thy gath'ring fleets
O'erspread the sea, and stop up ev'ry port;
Cato shall open to himself a passage,
And mock thy hopes.——

Portius. Oh, sir! forgive your son,
Whose grief hangs heavy on him. Oh, my
    father!
How am I sure it is not the last time
I e'er shall call you so? Be not displeased,
Oh, be not angry with me whilst I weep,
And, in the anguish of my heart, beseech you
To quit the dreadful purpose of your soul!

Cato. Thou hast been ever good and dutiful.

[*Embracing him.*

Weep not, my son, all will be well again;
The righteous gods, whom I have sought to
    please,
Will succour Cato, and preserve his
    children.

Portius. Your words give comfort to my
    drooping heart.

Cato. Portius, thou may'st rely upon my
    conduct:

Thy father will not act what misbecomes
   him.
But go, my son, and see if aught be wanting
Among thy father's friends; see them
   embark'd,
And tell me if the winds and seas befriend
   them.
My soul is quite weigh'd down with care,
   and asks
The soft refreshment of a moment's sleep.

Portius. My thoughts are more at ease, my
   heart revives—

[*Exit* Cato.

Enter Marcia.

Oh, Marcia! Oh, my sister, still there's hope
Our father will not cast away a life
So needful to us all, and to his country.
He is retired to rest, and seems to cherish
Thoughts full of peace.—He has dispatch'd
   me hence
With orders that bespeak a mind composed,
And studious for the safety of his friends.
Marcia, take care, that none disturb his
   slumbers.[*Exit.*

Marcia. Oh, ye immortal powers, that guard
   the just,
Watch round his couch, and soften his
   repose,
Banish his sorrows, and becalm his soul

With easy dreams; remember all his virtues,
And show mankind that goodness is your
    care!

Enter Lucia.

Lucia. Where is your father, Marcia; where is
    Cato?

Marcia. Lucia, speak low, he is retired to rest.
Lucia, I feel a gentle dawning hope
Rise in my soul—We shall be happy still.

Lucia. Alas, I tremble when I think on Cato!
In every view, in every thought, I tremble!
Cato is stern and awful as a god;
He knows not how to wink at human frailty,
Or pardon weakness, that he never felt.

Marcia. Though stern and awful to the foes
    of Rome,
He is all goodness, Lucia, always mild;
Compassionate and gentle to his friends;
Fill'd with domestic tenderness, the best,
The kindest father; I have ever found him
Easy and good, and bounteous to my wishes.

Lucia. 'Tis his consent alone can make us
    blest.
Marcia, we both are equally involved
In the same intricate, perplex'd distress.
The cruel hand of fate, that has destroy'd
Thy brother Marcus, whom we both
    lament——

Marcia. And ever shall lament; unhappy
  youth!

Lucia. Has set my soul at large, and now I
  stand
Loose of my vow. But who knows Cato's
  thoughts?
Who knows how yet he may dispose of
  Portius,
Or how he has determined of himself?

Marcia. Let him but live, commit the rest to
  Heav'n.

Enter Lucius.

Lucius. Sweet are the slumbers of the
  virtuous man!
Oh, Marcia, I have seen thy godlike father!
Some power invisible supports his soul,
And bears it up in all its wonted greatness.
A kind, refreshing sleep is fall'n upon him:
I saw him stretch'd at ease; his fancy lost
In pleasing dreams; as I drew near his
  couch,
He smiled, and cried, "Cæsar, thou canst not
  hurt me."

Marcia. His mind still labours with some
  dreadful thought.

Enter Juba.

Juba. Lucius, the horsemen are return'd from
    viewing
The number, strength, and posture of our
    foes,
Who now encamp within a short hour's
    march;
On the high point of yon bright western
    tower,
We ken them from afar; the setting sun
Plays on their shining arms and burnish'd
    helmets,
And covers all the field with gleams of fire.

Lucius. Marcia, 'tis time we should awake thy
    father.
Cæsar is still disposed to give us terms,
And waits at distance, till he hears from
    Cato.

Enter Portius.

Portius, thy looks speak somewhat of
    importance,
What tidings dost thou bring? Methinks,
    I see
Unusual gladness sparkle in thy eyes.

Portius. As I was hasting to the port,
    where now
My father's friends, impatient for a passage,
Accuse the ling'ring winds, a sail arrived
From Pompey's son, who, through the realms
    of Spain,
Calls out for vengeance on his father's death,

And rouses the whole nation up to arms.
Were Cato at their head, once more
    might Rome
Assert her rights, and claim her liberty.
But, hark! what means that groan?——Oh,
    give me way,
And let me fly into my father's presence![*Exit.*

Lucius. Cato, amidst his slumbers, thinks on
    Rome,
And, in the wild disorder of his soul,
Mourns o'er his country.—Ha! a second
    groan—
Heav'n guard us all!

Marcia. Alas, 'tis not the voice
Of one who sleeps; 'tis agonizing pain—
'Tis death is in that sound——

Enter Portius.

Portius. Oh, sight of woe!
Oh, Marcia, what we fear'd is come to pass—
Cato has fall'n upon his sword——

Lucius. Oh, Portius,
Hide all the horrors of thy mournful tale,
And let me guess the rest.

Portius. I've raised him up,
And placed him in his chair; where pale and
    faint,
He gasps for breath, and, as his life flows
    from him,

Demands to see his friends. His servants
   weeping,
Obsequious to his order, bear him hither!
———

Marcia. Oh, Heav'n! assist me in this dreadful
   hour,
To pay the last sad duties to my father!

    Cato *brought on, in a Chair.*

Cato. Here set me down——
Portius, come near me—Are my friends
   embark'd?
Can any thing be thought of for their
   service?
Whilst I yet live, let me not live in vain——
Oh, Lucius, art thou here?—Thou art too
   good—
Let this our friendship live between our
   children;
Make Portius happy in thy daughter
   Lucia——
Marcia, my daughter——
Oh, bend me forward!——Juba loves thee,
   Marcia—
A senator of Rome, while Rome survived,
Would not have match'd his daughter with a
   king—
But Cæsar's arms have thrown down all
   distinction—
I'm sick to death——Oh, when shall I get
   loose

From this vain world, th' abode of guilt and
    sorrow!
And yet, methinks, a beam of light breaks in
On my departing soul——Alas, I fear
I've been too hasty!—Oh, ye powers, that
    search
The heart of man, and weigh his inmost
    thoughts,
If I have done amiss, impute it not——
The best may err, but you are good, and—
    Oh!—[*Dies.*

Portius. There fled the greatest soul that ever
    warm'd
A Roman breast:—
From hence, let fierce contending nations
    know,
What dire effects from civil discord flow:
'Tis this that shakes our country with alarms;
And gives up Rome a prey to Roman arms;
Produces fraud, and cruelty, and strife,
And robs the guilty world of Cato's life.
    [*Exeunt omnes.*